Songs of Love, Moon, & Wind

Poems from the Chinese

D0448659

ALSO BY KENNETH REXROTH

WRITTEN ON THE SKY
Poems from the Japanese

Songs of Love, Moon, & Wind

Poems from the Chinese

Translated by
Kenneth Rexroth

SELECTED BY ELIOT WEINBERGER

A NEW DIRECTIONS BOOK

Copyright © 1970, 1971 by **KENNETH REXROTH**.
Copyright © 1972 by **KENNETH REXROTH** and **LING CHUNG**
Copyright © 2009 by **NEW DIRECTIONS PUBLISHING CORPORATION**

All rights reserved. Except for brief passages quoted in a newspaper, magazine, radio, or television review, no part of this book may be reproduced in any form or by any means, electronic or mechanical, including photocopying and recording, or by any information storage and retrieval system, without permission in writing from the Publisher.

Cover and Interior Design by **HSU + ASSOCIATES**
Cover image inspired by **MICHAEL WONG/THE TEA GALLERY, NEW YORK**
Manufactured in the **UNITED STATES OF AMERICA**
New Directions Books are printed on acid-free paper.
First published by New Directions as New Directions Paperbook (NDP1149) in 2009
Published simultaneously in Canada by **PENGUIN BOOKS CANADA LIMITED**

Library of Congress Cataloging-in-Publication Data:

Songs of love, moon, and wind : poems from the Chinese / translated by Kenneth Rexroth ; selected by Eliot Weinberger.—1st American paperback ed.
    p. cm.
  "First published by New Directions as New Directions Paperbook (NDP1149) in 2009; published simultaneously in Canada by Penguin Books Canada Limited."
  ISBN 978-0-8112-1836-8 (paperbook : alk. paper)
  1. Chinese poetry—Translations into English. I. Rexroth, Kenneth, 1905-1982. II. Weinberger, Eliot. III. Title: Poems from the Chinese.
  PL2658.E3S6646 2009
  895.1'1008—dc22

                            2008050557

NEW DIRECTIONS BOOKS are published for James Laughlin
by New Directions Publishing Corporation
80 Eighth Avenue, New York, NY 10011

TABLE OF CONTENTS

WRITTEN ON THE WALL AT
CHANG'S HERMITAGE

It is Spring in the mountains.
I come alone seeking you.
The sound of chopping wood echoes
Between the silent peaks.
The streams are still icy.
There is snow on the trail.
At sunset I reach your grove
In the stony mountain pass.
You want nothing, although at night
You can see the aura of gold
And silver ore all around you.
You have learned to be gentle
As the mountain deer you have tamed.
The way back forgotten, hidden
Away, I become like you,
An empty boat, floating, adrift.

TU FU

杜
甫

TO A TRAVELER

Last year when I accompanied you
As far as the Yang Chou Gate,
The snow was flying, like white willow cotton.
This year, Spring has come again,
And the willow cotton is like snow.
But you have not come back.
Alone before the open window,
I raise my wine cup to the shining moon.
The wind, moist with evening dew,
Blows the gauze curtains.
Maybe Chang-O, the moon goddess,
Will pity this single swallow
And join us together with the cord of light
That reaches beneath the painted eaves of your home.

SU TUNG-P'O

蘇
東
坡

THE TRAIL UP WU GORGE

The trail climbs in zigzags
High above spiralling whirlpools.
Swift waters break against sheer rocks.
On the evening breeze comes the sound
Of a boy playing his flute,
Riding home on the back of an ox.
The last drops of rain mingle
With the cloud of my horse's breath.
New grass grows on the ancient ramparts.
On the abandoned monuments
The old inscriptions are lost in time.
I am bound on a journey without end,
And cannot bear the song of the cuckoo.

SUN YÜN-FENG

孫
雲
鳳

3

BITTER COLD

Bitter cold. No one is abroad.
I have been looking everywhere for you.
If you don't believe me,
Look at my footprints in the snow.

ANONYMOUS
(SIX DYNASTIES)

匿
名
六
朝

AUTUMN

A cup of clear wine
Sweet as honey.
A girl with braids
Black as a crow,
Why ask if Spring
Is lovelier than Autumn?
I have never been able
To decide if peach blossoms
Were prettier than chrysanthemums

CH'IN KUAN

秦
觀

ON SPRING

I idle at the window
In the small garden.
The Spring colors are bright.
Inside, the curtains have not been raised
And the room is deep in shadow.
In my high chamber
I silently play my jade zither.
Far-off mountain caves spit clouds,
Hastening the coming of dusk.
A light breeze brings puffs of rain
And casts moving shadows on the ground.
I am afraid I cannot keep
The pear blossoms from withering.

LI CH'ING-CHAO

李
清
照

THOUGHTS IN EXILE

I lift my head and watch
The phoenix and the snowy swan
Cross the heavens in their migrations.
Wealth, office, position,
After all these years, mean nothing to me.
The foundered horse no longer
Hopes to travel a thousand miles.
In exile, in Autumn,
I grow lazy and indifferent.
In history men have
Always been treated like this.
I am forbidden to visit the Western Lake.
There is no place else I want to go.
The wise man, no matter how he is treated,
Knows that Heaven does nothing without reason.
But nobody can stop me
From writing poems about the
Mountains and rivers of Wu.

SU TUNG-P'O

蘇
東
坡

EVENING IN THE VILLAGE

Here in the mountain village
Evening falls peacefully.
Half tipsy, I lounge in the
Doorway. The moon shines in the
Twilit sky. The breeze is so
Gentle the water is hardly
Ruffled. I have escaped from
Lies and trouble. I no longer
Have any importance. I
Do not miss my horses and
Chariots. Here at home I
Have plenty of pigs and chickens.

LU YU

陸
游

VISIT TO THE HERMIT TS'UI

Moss covered paths between scarlet peonies,
Pale jade mountains fill your rustic windows.
I envy you, drunk with flowers,
Butterflies swirling in your dreams.

CH'IEN CH'I

錢
起

THE TURNING YEAR

Nightfall. Clouds scatter and vanish.
The sky is pure and cold.
Silently the River of Heaven turns in the Jade Vault.
If tonight I do not enjoy life to the full,
Next month, next year, who knows where I will be?

SU TUNG-P'O

蘇
東
坡

TO PI SSU YAO

We have talent. People call us
The leading poets of our day.
Too bad, our homes are humble,
Our recognition trivial.
Hungry, ill clothed, servants treat
Us with contempt. In the prime
Of life, our faces are wrinkled.
Who cares about either of us,
Or our troubles? We are our own
Audience. We appreciate
Each other's literary
Merits. Our poems will be handed
Down along with great dead poets'.
We can console each other.
At least we shall have descendants.

TU FU

杜
甫

11

JOY OF WINE

I remember in Hsi T'ing
All the many times
We got lost in the sunset,
Happy with wine,
And could not find our way back.
When the evening came,
Exhausted with pleasure,
We turned our boat.
By mistake we found ourselves even deeper
In the clusters of lotus blossoms,
And startled the gulls and egrets
From the sand bars.
They crowded into the air
And hastily flapped away
To the opposite shore.

LI CH'ING-CHAO

李
清
照

AN EXCUSE FOR NOT RETURNING THE
VISIT OF A FRIEND

Do not be offended because
I am slow to go out. You know
Me too well for that. On my lap
I hold my little girl. At my
Knees stands my handsome little son.
One has just begun to talk.
The other chatters without
Stopping. They hang on my clothes
And follow my every step.
I can't get any farther
Than the door. I am afraid
I will never make it to your house.

MEI YAO-CH'EN

梅
堯
臣

FAREWELL TO SHEN YUEH

Heading East or West, down the
Many years, how often we
Have separated here at
Lo Yang Gate. Once when I left
The snowflakes seemed like flower
Petals. Now today the petals
Seem like snow.

FAN YUN

范
雲

COUNTRY COTTAGE

A peasant's shack beside the
Clear river, the rustic gate
Opens on a deserted road.
Weeds grow over the public well.
I loaf in my old clothes. Willow
Branches sway. Flowering trees
Perfume the air. The sun sets
Behind a flock of cormorants,
Drying their black wings along the pier.

TU FU

杜
甫

TO THE TUNE "GLITTERING SWORD HILTS"

I have always been sorry
Our words were so trivial
And never matched the depths
Of our thoughts. This morning
Our eyes met,
And a hundred emotions
Rushed through our veins.

LIU YÜ-HSI

劉
禹
錫

IN THE EVENING I WALK BY THE RIVER

The frozen river is drifted deep with snow.
For days, only a few spots near the bank have stayed
    open.
In the evening when everyone has gone home,
The cormorants roost on the boats of the fishermen.

OU-YANG HSIU

歐
陽
修

DEEP NIGHT

Deep night. I cannot sleep.
I get up and sing softly to my lute.
Moonlight glows in the gauze curtains.
I open my nightgown, and let
The fresh night air bathe my body.
A lonely wild goose cries out
In the distant meadow.
A night bird flies calling through the trees.
I come and go without rest.
What do I gain by it?
My mind is distracted by worries
That will never cease.
My heart is all bruised
By the troubled ghosts who haunt it.

JUAN CHI

阮
籍

DAWN OVER THE MOUNTAINS

The city is silent,
Sound drains away,
Buildings vanish in the light of dawn,
Cold sunlight comes on the highest peak,
The thick dust of night
Clings to the hills,
The earth opens,
The river boats are vague,
The still sky—
The sound of falling leaves.
A huge doe comes to the garden gate,
Lost from the herd,
Seeking its fellows.

TU FU

杜
甫

THE MORNING SUN SHINES

The morning sun shines
Through the filigree shutters.
A wind full of light
Blows open her thin gauze robe.
A sly smile comes on her lips.
Her moth eyebrows arch
Over her beautiful eyes.

EMPEROR WU OF LIANG

梁
武
帝

WHEN THE PLUMS BY
THE BACK PAVILION BLOOMED

Frail as thin jade, perfume thick as sandalwood
Deep in the still melting snow—
This year I hate to visit the late-blooming plums.

He is in the South in the second story of an inn by the
    river.
Clouds and mist stretch far over the water.

I am here, in the long clear weather
Leaning against the balustrade
With the kingfisher-green curtain rolled low.

A guest comes. We fill our wine cups
And sing together. Here too the water flows into the
    clouds.
We should cut the sunlit branches of blossoms
And not wait until the Tatar flute
Sounds from the West Tower.

LI CH'ING-CHAO

李
清
照

ON HIS THIRTY-THIRD BIRTHDAY

More than thirty years have rushed
By me like a runaway
Chariot. I too have spent
My life rushing here and there
From one end of the country
To the other. I long for
The homestead where I was born,
A thousand mountain ranges
Away. Like yellow leaves in
The decline of Summer a
Few white hairs have already
Appeared on my head. All my
Travels only made tracks
In drifting sand. I piled up
Learning like a snowball.
I crossed mountains and passed
Examinations and gave
Learned speeches. What did I gain?
Better I stayed home
And raised prize melons.

TSENG KUO-FAN

REMORSE

Deep in the silent inner room

Every fiber of my soft heart

Turns to a thousand strands of sorrow.

I loved the Spring,

But the Spring is gone

As rain hastens the falling petals.

I lean on the balustrade,

Moving from one end to the other.

My emotions are still disordered.

Where is he?

Withered grass stretches to the horizon

And hides from sight

Any road by which he might return.

LI CH'ING-CHAO

李
清
照

THE FARM BY THE LAKE

For ten miles the mountains rise
Above the lake. The beauty
Of water and mountain is
Impossible to describe.
In the glow of evening
A traveler sits in front
Of an inn, sipping wine.
The moon shines above a
Little bridge and a single
Fisherman. Around the farm
A bamboo fence descends to
The water. I chat with an
Old man about work and crops.
Maybe, when the years have come
When I can lay aside my
Cap and robe of office,
I can take a little boat
And come back to this place.

CHU HSI

朱
熹

NIGHT THOUGHTS WHILE TRAVELING

A light breeze rustles the reeds
Along the riverbanks. The
Mast of my lonely boat soars
Into the night. Stars blossom
Over the vast desert of
Waters. Moonlight flows on the
Surging river. My poems have
Made me famous but I grow
Old, ill and tired, blown hither
And yon; I am like a gull
Lost between heaven and earth.

TU FU

杜
甫

SPRING JOY

Drafty winds and fine rain
Make a chilly Spring.
I drink wine, remembering bygone happiness,
Under the pear blossoms,
Weeping with misery.
Through the scented grasses
And broken mists, we walked
Along the southern bank of the river,
Tears of farewell
Blurring the distant mountains.
Last night I was fulfilled in a dream.
Speechless, we made love
In mist and clouds.
Alas, when I awoke
The old agony returned.
I tossed in my quilt
Angry at my own helplessness.
It is easier to see Heaven
Than to see you.

CHU SHU-CHEN

朱
淑
真

TWO SPRINGS

Spring has come to the women's quarter.
Once more the new grass is kingfisher green.
The cracked red buds of plum blossoms
Are still unopened little balls.
Blue-green clouds carve jade dragons.
The jade powder becomes fine dust.
I try to hold on to my morning dream.
I have already drained and broken
The cup of Spring.
Flower shadows lie heavy
On the garden gate.
In the orange twilight
Pale moonlight spreads
On the translucent curtain.
Three times in two years
My lord has gone away to the East.
Today he returns,
And my joy is already
Greater than the Spring.

LI CH'ING-CHAO

李
清
照

27

FISHERMAN

The wind blows the line out from his fishing pole.
In a straw hat and grass cape the fisherman
Is invisible in the long reeds.
In the fine Spring rain it is impossible to see very far
And the mist rising from the water has hidden the hills.

OU-YANG HSIU

歐
陽
修

FAREWELL ONCE MORE

Here we part.
You go off in the distance,
And once more the forested mountains
Are empty, unfriendly.
What holiday will see us
Drunk together again?
Last night we walked
Arm in arm in the moonlight,
Singing sentimental ballads
Along the banks of the river.
Your honor outlasts three emperors.
I go back to my lonely house by the river,
Mute, friendless, feeding the crumbling years.

TU FU

杜
甫

NIGHT WITHOUT END

Night without end. I cannot sleep.
The full moon blazes overhead.
Far off in the night I hear someone call.
Hopelessly I answer, "Yes."

ANONYMOUS
(SIX DYNASTIES)

匿
名
六
朝

ALONE

I raise the curtains and go out
To watch the moon. Leaning on the
Balcony, I breathe the evening
Wind from the West, heavy with the
Odors of decaying Autumn.
The rose jade of the river
Blends with the green jade of the void
Hidden in the grass a cricket chirps.
Hidden in the sky storks cry out.
I turn over and over in
My heart the memories of
Other days. Tonight as always
There is no one to share my thoughts.

CHU SHU-CHEN

朱
淑
真

SEVENTH DAY SEVENTH MONTH

We lie one against the other,
Tangle together like painted
Clouds on a screen, then,
Thighs enlaced, heads together
On the pillow we sing softly
To the full moon and watch time pass.
The declining moon marks the hours.
Suddenly we are seized by grief and fear.
Three o'clock in the morning
Has gone by but we cannot
Get enough of one another. Insatiable
Passion, night swift as the shuttle
In the loom. Oh Heaven, what is
Your price for one more hour?

KUAN YUN-SHIH

貫
雲
石

SORROW OF DEPARTURE

Red lotus incense fades on
The jeweled curtain. Autumn
Comes again. Gently I open
My silk dress and float alone
On the orchid boat. Who can
Take a letter beyond the clouds?
Only the wild geese come back
And write their ideograms
On the sky under the full
Moon that floods the West Chamber.
Flowers, after their kind, flutter
And scatter. Water after
Its nature, when spilt, at last
Gathers again in one place.
Creatures of the same species
Long for each other. But we
Are far apart and I have
Grown learned in sorrow.
Nothing can make it dissolve
And go away. One moment,
It is on my eyebrows.
The next, it weighs on my heart.

LI CH'ING-CHAO

李
清
照

33

A MOUNTAIN SPRING

There is a brook in the mountains,
Nobody I ask knows its name.
It shines on the earth like a piece
Of the sky. It falls away
In waterfalls, with a sound
Like rain. It twists between rocks
And makes deep pools. It divides
Into islands. It flows through
Calm reaches. It goes its way
With no one to mind it. The years
Go by, its clear depths never change.

CH'U KUANG-HSI

儲
光
羲

TRAVELING NORTHWARD

Screech owls moan in the yellowing
Mulberry trees. Field mice scurry,
Preparing their holes for Winter.
Midnight, we cross an old battlefield.
The moonlight shines cold on white bones.

TU FU

杜
甫

THE END OF THE YEAR

When a friend starts on a journey of a thousand miles,
As he is about to leave, he delays again and again.
When men part, they feel they may never meet again.
When a year has gone, how will you ever find it again?
I wonder where it has gone, this year that is ended?
Certainly someplace far beyond the horizon.
It is gone like a river which flows to the East,
And empties into the sea without hope of return.
My neighbors on the left are heating wine.
On the right they are roasting a fat pig.
They will have one day of joy
As recompense for a whole year of trouble.
We leave the bygone year without regret.
Will we leave so carelessly the years to come?
Everything passes, everything
Goes, and never looks back,
And we grow older and less strong.

SU TUNG-P'O

蘇
東
坡

TO THE TUNE "THE FAIR MAID OF YU"

Once when young I lay and listened
To the rain falling on the roof
Of a brothel. The candlelight
Gleamed on silk and silky flesh.
Later I heard it on the
Cabin roof of a small boat
On the Great River, under
Low clouds, where wild geese cried out
On the Autumn storm. Now I
Hear it again on the monastery
Roof. My hair has turned white.
Joy—sorrow—parting—meeting—
Are all as though they had
Never been. Only the rain
Is the same, falling in streams
On the tiles, all through the night.

CHIANG CHIEH

蔣
捷

PLAINT

Spring flowers, Autumn moons,
Water lilies still carry
Away my heart like a lost
Boat. As long as I am flesh
And bone I will never find
Rest. There will never come a
Time when I will be able
To resist my emotions.

CHU SHU-CHEN

朱
淑
真

LONELINESS

A hawk hovers in air.

Two white gulls float on the stream.

Soaring with the wind, it is easy

To drop and seize

Birds who foolishly drift with the current.

Where the dew sparkles in the grass,

The spider's web waits for its prey.

The processes of nature resemble the business of men.

I stand alone with ten thousand sorrows.

TU FU

杜
甫

ALL YEAR LONG

1

We break off a branch of poplar catkins.
A hundred birds sing in the tree.
Lying beneath it in the garden,
We talk to each other,
Our tongues in each other's mouth.

2

The sultry air is heavy with flower perfumes.
What is there better to do this hot night
Than throw off the covers
And lie together naked?

3

A cold wind blows open the window.
The moon looks in, full and bright.
Not a sound,
Not a voice,
In the night.
Then from behind the bed curtains,
Two giggles.

4

A freezing sky.
The year ends.
Icy winds whirl the snowflakes.
Under the covers
My darling is hotter than midsummer night.

ANONYMOUS
(SIX DYNASTIES)

匿
名
六
朝

EAST WIND

The burgeoning trees are thick with leaves
The birds are singing on all the hills.
The East Wind blows softly.
The birds sing, the flowers dance.
This minor magistrate is drunk.
Tomorrow when he wakes up,
Spring will no longer be new.

OU-YANG HSIU

歐
陽
修

WATCHING LOTUSES

Wind comes on the lake.
The waves spread far and wide.
Already Autumn is ending.
The red lotus blossoms are few,
Their fragrance is sparse.
All men love the reflection in the water
Of the colored mountains
And never stop talking of their beauty.
The lotus pods are ripe.
The lotus leaves have turned old.
Duckweed and rushes are soaked with crystal dew.
Gulls and egrets along the bank
Have their heads tucked beneath their wings,
Or turn their heads away,
As if they too regret
That you must go back so soon.

LI CH'ING-CHAO

李
清
照

43

WHEN WILL I BE HOME?

When will I be home? I don't know.
In the mountains, in the rainy night,
The Autumn lake is flooded.
Someday we will be back together again.
We will sit in the candlelight by the West window,
And I will tell you how I remembered you
Tonight on the stormy mountain.

LI SHANG-YIN

李
商
隱

AUTUMN WIND

The Autumn wind blows white clouds
About the sky. Grass turns brown.
Leaves fall. Wild geese fly south.
The last flowers bloom, orchids
And chrysanthemums with their
Bitter perfume. I dream of
That beautiful face I can
Never forget. I go for
A trip on the river. The barge
Rides the current and dips with
The whitecapped waves. They play flutes
And drums, and the rowers sing.
I am happy for a moment
And then the old sorrow comes back.
I was young only a little while,
And now I am growing old.

EMPEROR WU OF HAN

漢
武
帝

SORROW

Heaven took my wife. Now it
Has also taken my son.
My eyes are not allowed a
Dry season. It is too much
For my heart. I long for death.
When the rain falls and enters
The earth, when a pearl drops into
The depth of the sea, you can
Dive in the sea and find the
Pearl, you can dig in the earth
And find the water. But no one
Has ever come back from the
Underground Springs. Once gone, life
Is over for good. My chest
Tightens against me. I have
No one to turn to. Nothing,
Not even a shadow in a mirror.

MEI YAO-CH'EN

梅
堯
臣

TO THE TUNE "IMMORTALS ON THE RIVERBANK"

How deep, profoundly deep, the courtyard is.
The windows are cloudy.
Fog penetrates the closed rooms.
Pussy willows and plum buds begin to show,
As Spring returns to the trees of Nanking.
I grow old in this old city.
Songs of love, moon, and wind are gone
With the past.
I am old and have accomplished little.
No one cares for me now.
I wither away like last year's
Scattered leaves.
I have no desire to light the lantern,
No desire to walk in the last snow.

LI CH'ING-CHAO

李
清
照

TO AN OLD TUNE

Men hope to last a hundred years.

Flowers last just for a Spring.

Just one day of wind and rain,

And they are scattered on the earth.

If they knew what was happening to them,

They would be as miserable as men.

LU KUEI-MENG

陸
龜
蒙

I WALK OUT INTO THE COUNTRY AT NIGHT

The moon is so high it is
Almost in the Great Bear.
I walk out of the city
Along the road to the West.
The damp wind ruffles my coat.
Dewy grass soaks my sandals.
Fishermen are singing
On the distant river.
Fox fires dance on the ruined tombs.
A chill wind rises and fills
Me with melancholy. I
Try to think of words that will
Capture the uncanny solitude.
I come home late. The night
Is half spent. I stand for a
Long while in the doorway.
My young son is still up, reading.
Suddenly he bursts out laughing,
And all the sadness of the
Twilight of my life is gone.

LU YU

陸
游

49

TO AN OLD TUNE

In my young days I never
Tasted sorrow. I wanted
To become a famous poet.
I wanted to get ahead
So I pretended to be sad.
Now I am old and have known
The depths of every sorrow,
And I am content to loaf
And enjoy the clear Autumn.

HSIN CH'I-CHI

辛
棄
疾

VISITORS

I have had asthma for a
Long time. It seems to improve
Here in this house by the river.
It is quiet too. No crowds
Bother me. I am brighter
And more rested. I am happy here.
When someone calls at my thatched hut
My son brings me my straw hat
And I go out and gather
A handful of fresh vegetables.
It isn't much to offer.
But it is given in friendship.

TU FU

杜
甫

MARRIED LOVE

You and I
Have so much love,
That it
Burns like a fire,
In which we bake a lump of clay
Molded into a figure of you
And a figure of me.
Then we take both of them,
And break them into pieces,
And mix the pieces with water,
And mold again a figure of you,
And a figure of me.
I am in your clay.
You are in my clay.
In life we share a single quilt.
In death we will share one coffin.

KUAN TAO-SHENG

管
道
升

CLEAR EVENING AFTER RAIN

The sun sinks towards the horizon.
The light clouds are blown away.
A rainbow shines on the river.
The last raindrops spatter the rocks.
Cranes and herons soar in the sky.
Fat bears feed along the banks.
I wait here for the West Wind
And enjoy the crescent moon
Shining through misty bamboos.

TU FU

杜
甫

RAIN ON THE RIVER

In the fog we drift hither
And yon over the dark waves.
At last our little boat finds
Shelter under a willow bank.
At midnight I am awake,
Heavy with wine. The smoky
Lamp is still burning. The rain
Is still sighing in the bamboo
Thatch of the cabin of the boat.

LU YU

陸
游

SPRING FADES

Spring fades. Why should I suffer so much from
   homesickness?
I am ill. Combing my long hair exasperates me.
Under the roof beams the swallows chatter too much
   all day long.
A soft breeze fills the curtains with the perfume of
   roses.

LI CH'ING-CHAO

李
清
照

A DREAM AT NIGHT

In broad daylight I dream I
Am with her. At night I dream
She is still at my side. She
Carries her kit of colored
Threads. I see her image bent
Over her bag of silks. She
Mends and alters my clothes and
Worries for fear I might look
Worn and ragged. Dead, she watches
Over my life. Her constant
Memory draws me towards death.

MEI YAO-CH'EN

梅
堯
臣

TO WEI PA, A RETIRED SCHOLAR

The lives of many men are
Shorter than the years since we have
Seen each other. Aldebaran
And Antares move as we have.
And now, what night is this? We sit
Here together in the candle
Light. How much longer will our prime
Last? Our temples are already
Grey. I visit my old friends.
Half of them have become ghosts.
Fear and sorrow choke me and burn
My bowels. I never dreamed I would
Come this way, after twenty years,
A wayfarer to your parlor.
When we parted years ago,
You were unmarried. Now you have
A row of boys and girls, who smile
And ask me about my travels.
How have I reached this time and place?
Before I can come to the end
Of an endless tale, the children
Have brought out the wine. We go
Out in the night and cut young
Onions in the rainy darkness.

We eat them with hot, steaming,
Yellow millet. You say, "It is
Sad, meeting each other again."
We drink ten toasts rapidly from
The rhinoceros horn cups.
Ten cups, and still we are not drunk.
We still love each other as
We did when we were schoolboys.
Tomorrow morning mountain peaks
Will come between us, and with them
The endless, oblivious
Business of the world.

TU FU

杜
甫

SUMMER DAY

Reading in the heat of noon
I grow sleepy, put my head
On my arms and fall asleep.
I forget to close the window
And the warm air blows in
And covers my body with petals.

YUAN MEI

袁
枚

WHAT IS THE MATTER WITH ME?

What is the matter with me?
With all the men in the world,
Why can I think only of you?

ANONYMOUS
(SIX DYNASTIES)

匿
名
六
朝

EPIGRAM

I fish for minnows in the lake.
Just born, they have no fear of man.
And those who have learned,
Never come back to warn them.

SU TUNG-P'O

蘇
東
坡

BRIMMING WATER

Under my feet the moon
Glides along the river.
Near midnight, a gusty lantern
Shines in the heart of night.
Along the sandbars flocks
Of white egrets roost,
Each one clenched like a fist.
In the wake of my barge
The fish leap, cut the water,
And dive and splash.

TU FU

杜
甫

RAIN IN THE ASPENS

My neighbor to the East has
A grove of aspens. Tonight
The rain sounds mournfully in
Them. Alone, at my window,
I cannot sleep. Autumn insects
Swarm, attracted by my light.

SU TUNG-P'O

蘇
東
坡

SINCE YOU WENT AWAY

After you were gone
The moon came and shone
In the vacant window.
I thought of you as a flower
Carried off by the wind,
That went its way,
And can never turn back.

SHU CH'I-SIANG

書
啟
翔

BY T'ING YANG WATERFALL

A strange, beautiful girl
Bathes her white feet in the flowing water.
The white moon, in the midst of the clouds,
Is far away, beyond the reach of man.

HSIEH LING-YÜN

謝
靈
運

SNOW STORM

Tumult, weeping, many new ghosts.
Heartbroken, aging, alone, I sing
To myself. Ragged mist settles
In the spreading dusk. Snow skurries
In the coiling wind. The wineglass
Is spilled. The bottle is empty.
The fire has gone out in the stove.
Everywhere men speak in whispers.
I brood on the uselessness of letters.

TU FU

杜
甫

TO THE TUNE "THE BODHISATTVA'S HEADDRESS"

The cries of returning wild geese
Are stilled as the strands of the cloud
Turn blue-green.
Snow falls outside the windows
Of the women's quarters.
The incense smoke rises straight up.
My phoenix hairpins glitter in the candlelight.
A tiny gold pendant in the shape of a lady
Swings under the beak of the phoenix.

Bugles sound. Dawn comes. Drums beat the watch.
The stars in the River of Heaven pale in the dawn.
I long for the Spring
And search for the first flowers,
But the West Wind is still as cold as ever.

LI CH'ING-CHAO

李
清
照

GREEN JADE PLUM TREES IN SPRING

Spring comes early to the gardens
Of the South, with dancing flowers.
The gentle breeze carries the sound
Of horses whinnying. The blue
Green plums are already as large
As beans. The willow leaves are long,
And really are curved like a girl's
Eyebrows. Butterflies whirl in the
Long sunlight. In the evening the
Mist lies heavy on the flowers.
The grass is covered with dew.
Girls in their transparent dresses,
Indolent and lascivious,
Lounge in their hammocks. Swallows, two
By two, nest under the painted eaves.

OU'YANG HSIU

歐
陽
修

THE WILLOW

My neighbor's willow sways its frail
Branches, graceful as a girl of
Fifteen. I am sad because this
Morning the violent
Wind broke its longest bough.

TU FU

杜
甫

69

WRITTEN BY CHANCE

Fifteen years ago, beneath moonlight and flowers,
I walked with you—
We composed flower-viewing poems together.
Tonight the moonlight and flowers are just the same
But how can I ever hold in my arms the same love.

LI CH'ING-CHAO

李
清
照

I PASS THE NIGHT AT
GENERAL HEADQUARTERS

A clear night in harvest time.

In the courtyard at headquarters

The wu-tung trees grow cold.

In the city by the river

I wake alone by a guttering

Candle. All night long bugle

Calls disturb my thoughts. The splendor

Of the moonlight floods the sky.

Who bothers to look at it?

Whirlwinds of dust, I cannot write.

The frontier pass is unguarded.

It is dangerous to travel.

Ten years wandering, sick at heart.

I perch here like a bird on a

Twig, thankful for a moment's peace.

TU FU

杜
甫

SPRING ENDS

The gentle breeze has died down
The perfumed dust has settled.
It is the end of the time
Of flowers. Evening falls
And all day I have been too
Lazy to comb my hair.
Our furniture is just the same.
He no longer exists.
All effort would be wasted.
Before I can speak,
My tears choke me.
I hear that Spring at Two Rivers
Is still beautiful.
I had hoped to take a boat there,
But I know so fragile a vessel
Won't bear such a weight of sorrow.

LI CH'ING-CHAO

李
清
照

MOON FESTIVAL

The Autumn constellations
Begin to rise. The brilliant
Moonlight shines on the crowds.
The moon toad swims in the river
And does not drown. The moon rabbit
Pounds the bitter herbs of the
Elixir of eternal life.
His drug only makes my heart
More bitter. The silver brilliance
Only makes my hair more white.
I know that the country is
Overrun with war. The moonlight
Means nothing to the soldiers
Camped in the western deserts.

TU FU

杜
甫

A RESTLESS NIGHT IN CAMP

In the penetrating damp
I sleep under the bamboos,
Under the penetrating
Moonlight in the wilderness.
The thick dew turns to fine mist.
One by one the stars go out.
Only the fireflies are left.
Birds cry over the water.
War breeds its consequences.
It is useless to worry,
Wakeful while the long night goes.

TU FU

杜
甫

FLOWER PETALS DRIFT
OVER THE COURTYARD

Flower petals drift over the courtyard

Moss creeps into the rooms

Everything was said on both sides

Now there is only a musty smell in the air.

WANG CH'ANG-LING

王
昌
齢

KILL THAT CROWING COCK

Kill that crowing cock.
Drive away the chattering birds.
Shoot the cawing crows.
I want this night to last
And morning never come back.
I don't want to see another dawn
For at least a year.

ANONYMOUS
(SIX DYNASTIES)

匿
名
六
朝

AUTUMN

It has turned cold.

The mountains grow more vast and more blue.

The Autumn waterfalls are louder.

I take my cane and go out the gate for a walk.

I can hear the last crickets

Singing in the chilly evening.

I am happy. The rays of the setting sun

Shine through the evening smoke

That hovers over the village.

I throw back my head,

Drunk with beauty,

And sing the "Willow Song"

At the top of my lungs.

WANG WEI

王
維

IDLENESS

I keep the rustic gate closed
For fear somebody might step
On the green moss. The sun grows
Warmer. You can tell it's Spring.
Once in a while, when the breeze
Shifts, I can hear the sounds of the
Village. My wife is reading
The classics. Now and then she
Asks me the meaning of a word.
I call for wine and my son
Fills my cup till it runs over.
I have only a little
Garden, but it is planted
With yellow and purple plums.

LU YU

陸
游

PLUM BLOSSOMS

The courtyard is deep, profoundly deep.
The windows are cloudy.
The rooms are foggy.
Spring is late.
For whom has my fragrant beauty withered?
Last night you appeared in my dreams.
The trees of the South must be all in bloom.
Frail as jade, ethereal as sandalwood perfume,
Our love will last always.
O Tatar flute on the South Tower
Do not blow.
You will blow away the rich perfume.
The wind grows warm
The sun shines longer.
We will be separated
Till the apricots bloom.

LI CH'ING-CHAO

李
清
照

STARS AND MOON ON THE RIVER

The Autumn night is clear
After the thunderstorm.
Venus glows on the river.
The Milky Way is white as snow.
The dark sky is vast and deep.
The Northern Crown sets in the dusk.
The moon like a clear mirror
Rises from the great void. When it
Has climbed high in the sky, moonlit
Frost glitters on the chrysanthemums.

TU FU

杜
甫

SPRING ENDS, II

Spring is over in the Imperial City.
Behind many doors, in my secluded garden
The grass is green in front of the staircase.

The wild geese have vanished from the evening sky.
From my high tower, who now will carry my message
  so far away?
My sorrow is drawn out, endless as silk floss.

Too much passion results in too many entanglements.
I can no longer get free from it.
Once more it is the Day of Cold Food.
The swings along the neighboring lanes are stilled.
People sit quietly watching the brilliant moon
Rise and drench the pear blossoms with its rays.

LI CH'ING-CHAO

李
清
照

TEA

By noon the heat became unbearable.
The birds stopped flying
And went to roost exhausted.
Sit here in the shade of the big tree.
Take off your hot woolen jacket.
The few small clouds floating overhead
Do nothing to cool the heat of the sun.
I'll put some tea on to boil
And cook some vegetables.
It's a good thing you don't live far.
You can stroll home after sunset.

CH'U KUANG-HSI

儲
光
羲

BY THE CITY GATE

A year ago today by
This very gate your face and
The peach blossoms mirrored each
Other. I do not know where
Your beautiful face has gone.
There are only peach blossoms
Flying in the Spring wind.

TS'UI HAO

崔
颢

THE SOUTHERN ROOM OVER THE RIVER

The room is prepared, the incense burned.
I close the shutters before I close my eyelids.
The patterns of the quilt repeat the waves of the river.
The gauze curtain is like a mist.
Then a dream comes to me and when I awake
I no longer know where I am.
I open the western window and watch the waves
Stretching on and on to the horizon.

SU TUNG-P'O

蘇
東
坡

A PRESENT FROM THE EMPEROR'S NEW CONCUBINE

I took a piece of the rare cloth of Ch'i,
White silk glowing and pure as frost on snow,
And made you a fan of harmony and joy,
As flawlessly round as the full moon.
Carry it always, nestled in your sleeve.
Wave it and it will make a cooling breeze.
I hope, that when Autumn comes back
And the North Wind drives away the heat,
You will not store it away amongst old gifts
And forget it, long before it is worn out.

LADY P'AN

班
婕
妤

INDEX

[Women poets are noted with an *.]